THE
PSALM 23
LIFE

THE
PSALM 23
LIFE

Experiencing the love of God
every day

David Knott

PELOS PRESS

Scripture quotations taken from The Holy Bible, New International Version® NIV®
Copyright © 1973 1978 1984 2011 by Biblica, Inc. TM
Used by permission. All rights reserved worldwide.

All emphases in Scripture quotations have been added by the author.

Cover design by: the author, using images by Karl Egger from Pixabay, and Nayyara Shabbir from Unsplash.

Published by PELOS PRESS
PELOS PRESS is the publishing arm of Quorn Creative Solutions Limited

ISBN-13: 9798669954055

Now may the God of peace, who through the blood of the eternal covenant brought back from the dead our Lord Jesus, that great Shepherd of the sheep, equip you with everything good for doing his will, and may he work in us what is pleasing to him, through Jesus Christ, to whom be glory for ever and ever. Amen.

HEBREWS 13:20-21

Contents

PREFACE

I wrote the first draft of this book before Covid-19 came and infected our world. Now that the foundations of life have been shaken, it seems to me that the truth, and comfort, declared by Psalm 23 for three thousand years is timely and much needed food for our souls.

Psalm 23 stands as an eternal testimony to the transforming power of God's love, and I hope to shine a new light upon that testimony, so that David's experience of God's love may become our experience too. The Psalm 23 Life opens the door to a life lived in joyful confidence and contentment, through experiencing the love of God every day.

I want to express my grateful appreciation to those who have helped in creating this book: to Karen for reading that first draft, and for her encouragement; to Leigh for his insights, and our stimulating lunchtime discussions; to Joy, not just for her generosity in reading two drafts, but for her deep insights and ideas; to Emily for her encouragement, observations and comments; to

Louise for her valuable assistance; and finally to Kathryn, not just for her brilliant editing skills, but also for her loving patience.

To them, and to you dear reader, I say, "May the Psalm 23 Life be yours in abundance."

LOOKING AT THE FAMILIAR WITH NEW EYES

Familiarity can be a good thing. We once went for a meal at the home of some friends who lived by a railway track. As we were all eating, there was a sudden blast of sound and vibration as a train thundered past. I looked up in surprise, only to be met by an even more surprising sight - our friends just carried on eating as if absolutely nothing had happened. I couldn't believe it, were they deaf? It then dawned on me that trains thundering past their house were so familiar to them that they didn't notice them anymore. If we lived by a railway track that level of familiarity would probably enable us to maintain our sanity, but if we want to hear God speak to us through familiar scriptures, then their very familiarity can be a problem.

"In more than 2 billion pageviews conducted by visitors to Bible Gateway during 2019" (1), six out of the eleven most popular Bible verses viewed were from Psalm 23 (2). Clearly, for many people, Psalm 23 is not only very popular but also precious.

In all honesty, although I was very familiar with Psalm 23, I would not say that it was precious to me, but then one night that changed. I was tossing and turning over a problem at work. My mind would not let it go. Even though mentally I laid it down at God's feet a number of times, it was as if my thoughts ignored me completely. Have you ever had times like that, when you want to stop thinking about something, but your thoughts seem to have a life of their own?

Then suddenly, out of nowhere, into my head came, "The Lord is my shepherd", and along with it came a deep sense of peace. That is when I decided to study Psalm 23, to teach from it at Church; and that is how this book came to be written.

I didn't know at the time, but a couple of weeks later, out of the blue, I was to lose my Dad. During that time Psalm 23 took on a very special significance. In times like that, the comfort and confidence that flow from trusting in our Heavenly Father are priceless. Psalm 23 is an eternal signpost to his constant, unshakeable, utterly reliable love and care for us, and its very familiarity helps us in times of need, but as with the train, that same familiarity can also cause its deep truths to skim across our minds rather than enter our hearts.

I have endeavoured to base all my thinking and writing on the belief that Psalm 23, along with all of the

Bible, was written under the inspiration of the Holy Spirit, and is therefore God's wholly reliable communication to us. That does not mean to say that careful study and account of context is not important - it certainly is, if we are to properly understand its meaning. I care deeply about meaning and understanding, because meaning, properly understood, is truth and truth sets us free. Or as Dallas Willard puts it, "Truth reveals reality, and reality can be described as what we humans run into when we are wrong." (3) Ultimately, my aim is only to express thoughts that arise from God's thoughts, those that he has chosen to reveal to us that is. You will need to judge for yourself how successful I have been, so let me encourage you to study the scriptures to see if my thoughts do indeed remain true to God's written word.

> *Making It Real:*
> *Of course, understanding alone is not enough. If we are to truly experience life in the fullness that God intends, then we need to put our understanding of the Bible into practice. It is acting upon our understanding of what God has said that will make our experience of him, and his love, real. And so, at various points in the book you will find short sections entitled "Making It Real", that highlight questions and applications for us.*

My hope and prayer is that our journey through Psalm 23 will help you look at the familiar with new eyes; that the journey will help you to more deeply understand, apply and experience its truths, and the reality they reveal... not just in the hard times, but in your everyday life. Such is the Psalm 23 life.

PSALM 23

The Lord is my shepherd, I shall not be in want.
　　He makes me lie down in green pastures,
he leads me beside quiet waters,
　　he restores my soul.
He guides me in paths of righteousness
　　for his name's sake.
Even though I walk
　　through the valley of the shadow of death,
I will fear no evil,
　　for you are with me;
your rod and your staff,
　　they comfort me.

You prepare a table before me
　　in the presence of my enemies.
You anoint my head with oil;
　　my cup overflows.
Surely goodness and love will follow me
　　all the days of my life,
and I will dwell in the house of the Lord
　　forever.

1. THE LORD IS MY SHEPHERD

The Lord is my shepherd… (Psalm 23:1)

Now this is a Psalm of David who, from his experience as a young shepherd boy, knew exactly what being a shepherd involved. We don't know when David wrote the Psalm, it is easy to imagine David writing it whilst watching over his Father's sheep, as he thought about how God's care for him was like his care for the sheep. But I agree with those who believe that David wrote Psalm 23 much later in life, because you get the sense that it is written by someone with battle scars, who had lived life, someone looking back on all the ways the Lord had rescued him, provided for him and cared for him. The key thing, I suppose, is that it was written by David out of his experience of life, and out of his experience of God, which makes Psalm 23 relevant to all ages and stages of life. It is for times of sorrow, yes, but also for times of goodness – goodness that follows me all the days of my life.

So let's look first at who our shepherd is, because David says "THE LORD is my shepherd." "The Lord" in Hebrew is the word Yahweh, which is the name by which God made himself known to the Israelites, and as you might expect, being the name of God, it is both mysterious and profound. In this name, God proclaimed himself to be the great "I AM". He proclaimed himself to be the reality behind all reality, the cause behind every cause, every event. It proclaimed him to be the entirely sovereign one, free from constraint, wholly free from dependence on anything outside of himself. Yahweh is the one who is essentially unnameable, inexplicable. He simply is. He is the absolute and unchangeable one. This is your shepherd. Your shepherd is all powerful, because he made all things; he's all knowing, because he knows the end from the beginning; he is outside of space and time – he made space and time. Without him nothing was made that has been made. How confident do you feel about your shepherd now?

Then there is the next word to consider, a very small but important word – "The Lord IS my shepherd." How different would we feel if it said, The Lord might be my shepherd? "Is" is such a definite word, it means that the Lord is my shepherd right now, at this moment in time. The maker of all things is your shepherd. Now it doesn't say that the Lord was my shepherd, as if somehow having gained him as my shepherd I could subsequently lose him as my shepherd. Neither does it say that the Lord will be my shepherd, as if I need to wait, live life on my own and then at some point in the future he will become my shepherd, perhaps on my death bed. No, it says the Lord IS my shepherd.

> *Making It Real:*
> *The Lord wants you to know that he is your shepherd now. And that means that there will never be a moment in your life when he is not your shepherd. All the days of your life you will be able to say, "The Lord IS my shepherd", whatever happens to you.*

MY SHEPHERD?

King David was able to say, "The Lord is MY shepherd", and you can't get more personal than that. There is no intermediary, no deputy – he is MY shepherd. David understood that God was his shepherd in an intimate and personal way. In David's time shepherds knew their sheep as individuals. They knew them each by name, and it is the same today in that part of the world. A shepherd in Lebanon was asked if he always counted his sheep each night to make sure they were all safe, and he said, no he didn't, so he was asked how he knew they were all safe. His answer was this, "Master if you were to put a cloth over my eyes, and bring me any sheep, and only let me put my hands on its face, I could tell you if it was one of my sheep or not." (4) And as a shepherd boy, David would have known his sheep as individuals too. He would have known their personalities and their habits, and as your shepherd the Lord knows you better than you know yourself. He does not know you only as one in a crowd, he knows you completely. In Psalm 139:1-4 he says this:

You have searched me, Lord,
    and you know me.
You know when I sit and when I rise;
    you perceive my thoughts from afar.
You discern my going out and my lying down;
    you are familiar with all my ways.
Before a word is on my tongue
    you, Lord, know it completely.

Making It Real:
The Lord is MY shepherd. But this raises an important question – is the Lord everyone's shepherd? David could say it, based on his relationship with God, but can you? The answer is this – the Lord is your shepherd if you know Jesus.

In John 10:14,15 Jesus said:

'I am the good shepherd, I know my sheep and my sheep know me – Just as the Father knows me and I know the Father – and I lay down my life for the sheep.'

Jesus demonstrated his right to be called the "good shepherd" by laying down his life for us. He did this by dying on the Cross for your sin and for mine. Now more than six hundred years before Jesus was born, Isaiah prophesied that Jesus would lay down his life for the sheep, and he also explained why:

But he was pierced for our transgressions, he was crushed for our iniquities; the punishment that brought us peace was on him, and by his wounds we are healed. We all like sheep, have gone astray, each of us has turned to our own way, and the Lord has laid on him the iniquity of us all. (Isaiah 53:5,6)

Each and every single one of us is like a sheep who has gone astray. We have done our own thing, we have ignored God's way and done things our own way. We have hurt other people, we have hurt ourselves and most importantly of all, we have offended almighty God, who out of justice must punish all wrong doing. BUT, because of his great love for us, God made a way to punish our sin by laying it upon Jesus. That is why Isaiah says, "he was pierced for our transgressions, he was crushed for our iniquities". So, because Jesus the Son of God suffered death on a cross, in my place, I have received forgiveness from God. The punishment that brought us peace, was laid on him. By his wounds we are healed.

When I was an engineering student, I didn't know any of this, I didn't even believe in God. I had decided that God did not exist, that science had made God redundant. But then a friend of mine became a Christian, and I could see a massive change in him that I could not explain. We had many conversations about what had happened to him and what it meant to be a Christian.

Two things stood out to me from these conversations. The first was that my "self-justification" was demolished. I said, "I don't believe in God, but even if there is a God, I'll be alright; I'm a good person; I don't go around mugging old ladies."

He replied, "Yes, but the Bible says that God is so perfect that all our righteous deeds are like filthy rags to him."

The second thing was when he told me that God wanted a relationship with me. Now this struck me as a big deal. Could this possibly be true? Could it be true that the creator of all things wanted a relationship with me?

After a few more conversations, I got to the point where I wanted to know if this was true or not. My thinking went something like this, "I don't know if God exists, but if he does, I would like a relationship with him, that's got to be amazing! I'll give this Christianity a go, and I'll soon find out if it is true or not."

So one day I sat in my car and read a booklet called "Journey Into Life". It explained about how we are all like sheep who have gone astray, about how my sin separated me from God, about how much God loves me, and about how Jesus had died for me so that I might be forgiven and have a relationship with him. At the end of the booklet was a prayer to pray if you wanted to give your life to God. When I got to the prayer, even then, I did not know if God was real, but I did know that I wanted to know him if he was. So I prayed the prayer, and meant it.

I did not expect what happened next: there were no angels singing; or lights in the sky; but, in a way that I cannot explain, I knew that God had entered my life; I knew that I could talk to him, and I did. I started asking for his help in what I was doing.

That was over forty years ago, and I can say that the Lord has been my shepherd ever since. David's testimony, as he expressed it in Psalm 23, has become my testimony, and it can become your testimony too.

> *Making It Real:*
> *So how do I make the Lord MY shepherd? By knowing Jesus the Son of God. And how do I come to know Jesus? By listening to his voice, and agreeing with him that I am a sheep who has gone astray; a sheep who needs forgiveness; a sheep who needs a saviour. Is Jesus speaking to you on this very point? Do you want to know him, do you want to ask him to be your shepherd? If you do, then here is a short prayer for you:*
> *Lord Jesus, thank you for showing me that I am a sheep who has gone astray. Thank you for taking my punishment and dying in my place. I trust in you, and you alone, to save me and forgive me. Please be my shepherd, and help me to follow you all the days of my life. Amen*

If you have prayed this prayer for the first time, please tell someone you know is a Christian, because, as we will see, when the Lord becomes your shepherd, that is just

25

the beginning. Right before he said that he was the good shepherd, Jesus also said:

> I have come that they may have life, and have it to the full. (John 10:10)

WHY A SHEPHERD?

Shepherds have a special place in the Bible. Abraham, Isaac and Jacob kept sheep. Joseph's family took their sheep to Egypt, even though the Egyptians despised shepherds. But God holds shepherds in high regard. Every Christmas we remember the special place that the shepherds had in the birth of our Lord Jesus. As Luke tells us, even though Bethlehem was so full of people that there was no room for Mary and Joseph to stay, who did the angels tell that a saviour had been born that very day, and that they would find him wrapped in cloths and lying in a manger? It was the shepherds. But why shepherds? Yes, they were in fields nearby, but there were many other people who would have been even closer, and yes they were awake, keeping watch over their flocks that night. But God could have woken anyone he wanted; a multitude of angels tends to have that effect on you. But God chose to reveal the birth of his Son to the shepherds because it is the heart of God to be a shepherd.

In Ezekiel 34:15-16 God says:

I myself will tend my sheep and make them lie down, declares the Sovereign Lord. I will search for the lost and bring back the strays. I will bind up the injured and strengthen the weak.

So then here are six things that, out of his shepherd heart, the Lord does for us:

1. He calls his sheep.
We've already looked at this. The only question really is: do I want to be his sheep?

2. He rescues his sheep.
The thing about sheep is that they have a tendency to wander off and get lost, and fall into trouble. And so do we. Just like in the parable of the lost sheep, our Lord Jesus seeks us when we get lost, and he brings back the strays. Sheep need someone to save them, from circumstances beyond their control, and even from themselves sometimes. We have a shepherd who is the saviour of the world, we can depend on him.

3. He leads his sheep.
You can't drive sheep as you do cattle; they must be led. The Eastern shepherds know their sheep by name and when they call them the sheep follow. In the East you will see the shepherd walking and the sheep following behind him. You see, even though they are incredibly dumb in many ways, there is one way in which sheep are really bright, and it is this - the sheep trust the shepherd. They know the shepherd well enough to trust that he

knows where the good food and water are, and they know themselves well enough to know that they don't. We can trust our Lord Jesus to lead us.

4. He protects his sheep.

Sheep have no defence against the thief who comes only to steal, kill and destroy, or against the wolf, the bear or the lion. But the shepherd protects his sheep from them, and from all the dangers that are too great for them. Whether the danger comes by day or by night, the shepherd will defend his sheep. The Lord, the maker of heaven and earth, is our defender, there is nothing and no one greater than him. So, relax, you are safe in his care.

5. He provides for his sheep.

He knows what they need before they do, and he knows where to find it. Is there any wonder that Jesus, the good shepherd, said:

'So do not worry, saying, "What shall we eat?" or "What shall we drink?" or "What shall we wear?" For the pagans run after all these things, and your heavenly Father knows that you need them. But seek first his kingdom and his righteousness, and all these things will be given to you as well.' (Matthew 6:31-33).

So do not worry, trust in your shepherd.

6. He cares for his sheep.

Sometimes sheep get hurt, they get sick, they get injured by thorns or any number of hazards in life, but the shepherd is always there to take care of them. And the Lord is always there to take care of you too. He binds you up when you are injured, he strengthens you when you are weak. There is a lovely picture of God's shepherding care in Isaiah 40:11…

He tends his flock like a shepherd: he gathers the lambs in his arms and carries them close to his heart; he gently leads those that have young.

Making It Real:
The Lord is your shepherd, so let me encourage you to do two things:
Think back over the last few months and thank God for how he has called you, rescued you, led you, protected you, provided for you and cared for you.
Ask yourself this, "What do I need my good shepherd to do for me?" And ask him to do it. It might be a need you have right now, or something that you can see coming in the future. But whatever it is you can face it with confidence, because if you know Jesus you can say, "The Lord is my shepherd."

2. I SHALL NOT BE IN WANT

… I shall not be in want.
He makes me lie down in green pastures,
he leads me beside quiet waters,
he restores my soul. (Psalm 23:1-3)

So we've looked at how the Lord, as our shepherd: calls us; rescues us; leads us; protects us; provides for us; and cares for us, in a very personal and individual way. Now, let's look in more detail at how the Lord does that for each and every one of his sheep. Psalm 23:1-3 says:

> The Lord is my shepherd, I shall not be in want.
>   He makes me lie down in green pastures,
> he leads me beside quiet waters,
>   he restores my soul.

"I shall not be in want" is a very definitive declaration by David, it leaves no room for doubt. He didn't say, "I usually don't want", or "I probably won't be in want", or even, "I hope I will not be in want". No, David's lifelong utter confidence and rock-solid trust in the Lord his shepherd is captured in these six short words, "I shall not be in want." Did it mean that he never suffered hardship, did it mean that he never suffered loss or disappointment or loneliness or pain? No, David's life is full of great blessing and victories, but it also contains times of crisis, like when he had to run for his life from King Saul, and hide in a cave with nothing, all alone. And there was the time when he had to pretend to be insane to escape Achish King of Gath. Later in his life, there came a time of great loss and distress for David and his men:

> When David and his men reached Ziklag, they found it destroyed by fire and their wives and sons and daughters taken captive. So David and his men wept aloud until they had no strength left to weep. David's two wives had been captured – Ahinoam of Jezreel and Abigail, the widow of Nabal of Carmel. David was greatly distressed because the men were talking of stoning him; each one was bitter in spirit because of his sons and daughters. But David found strength in the Lord his God. (1 Samuel 30:3-6)

And I guess that is the point. Having the Lord as your shepherd does not make you immune from trouble, loss and even great distress, but it does mean that you can always find strength in the Lord, as David did. By the way, because of the strength he found in the Lord, David and his men got back everything that had been taken; nothing was lost.

It is a recurring theme in the life of David for him to see the Lord as the only source of his strength. In Psalm 22:19 he declares:

But you, Lord, do not be far from me. You are my strength; come quickly to help me.

> *Making It Real:*
> *So here's a question for you. Do you need strength right now? Are you in a place that needs more courage, more patience, more persistence, more determination, more love, than you have in yourself to give? Then let David's prayer be your prayer, "Lord you are my strength, come quickly to help me".*

WANT?

So strength is something we need never be in want of, but "want" itself is an interesting word. It can have two meanings. Firstly, it can mean unfulfilled desire. We live in a society that is focused on nurturing and meeting our desires. We have an economy that is driven by our desires, and an advertising industry that is very skilled at making us want what we do not need. We want to have, we want to know, we want to control, we want... we want... Now the thing about want of this kind, these kinds of desires, is that there is no limit to them, because even when you get what you think you want, very soon you only want more. There is always that better car, that better house, that better job, that better handbag. And then there is the "want to know" which is an old desire, remember the "tree of the knowledge of good and evil" (Genesis 2:17), but the want to know is a desire that we have recently found a way to fulfil beyond the wildest imaginations of less than a generation ago. If we want to know something, we google it, but Google was only founded on 4th September 1998.

If we want to know what's happening in people's lives we go on social media. Social media is driven by the desire to know (and the desire to tell), to know the very latest news, the latest gossip, and meeting this want can consume us, it can eat up our time and energy.

Making It Real:
So let me just ask you, do you have your desire to know under control, or is your desire to know controlling you? If you wake up in a morning and the first thing you want to do is check your emails or go on social media to see what you've missed, then that has the hallmarks of an addiction. Indeed, our desire to be connected can be addictive, it can affect the brain like other addictions if we feed it. Have you ever considered fasting from your desire to be connected, your want to know? I would suggest that the more the thought of fasting from social

media for a day gives you a feeling of anxiety or strikes you with horror, the more you need to do it. I'm highlighting this need to know, because it is a relatively new potential addiction driven by technology, but whether it's a thirst for knowledge, or a thirst for drink, or a craving for a cigarette or a drug, if anything dominates our lives to that extent, we need to take action. Remember David's prayer "Lord you are my strength, come quickly to help me".

Now, the other meaning of want is lacking a necessity of life, and a better word for this kind of want is "need". When I was a student, many years ago, we learned about something called "Maslow's Hierarchy of Needs" (5), which basically identified that we all have a set of needs that motivate us.

Maslow's Hierarchy of Needs

When our most basic needs are met then we tend to turn our attention to meeting our higher needs. So:

1. Our most basic needs are physiological, we all need air, water, food and sleep.
2. Next, we all need safety, we need shelter, we need security, we need freedom from fear.
3. Next, we need to be loved and to belong, we need friends and family. In the west we are living in an epidemic of loneliness. This can affect us physiologically as well as emotionally. If your need for love and belonging is not being met then look around for a flock of the shepherd's sheep that will meet that need. But most of all remember that the shepherd's love for you endures forever, and that you belong to him.
4. Next, we have esteem needs, we need self-respect, achievement, independence.
5. And then finally at the top of the hierarchy of needs is this strange thing called "Self-Actualisation", which means that we all have a need to realise our full potential.

Of course, this hierarchy misses out our most important need of all, which is our need to be reconciled with God. But the point is that your shepherd will meet your every need, from the air that you breathe to the fulfilment of all the potential he created in you.

Making It Real:

Do you have a need that is not being met? Ask the Lord to meet your need, knowing that he knows what you need before you ask him.

Being in a Church or Christian fellowship will not only help you to meet your need for love and belonging, but also help you to reach your full potential. If these needs are not being met, then ask your shepherd to guide you to the group of Christians he has prepared for you. Not only has he prepared them for you, but he has also prepared you for them. He has made you to need them and them to need you. There are many different types of Church and Christian fellowship: large, small, formal, informal, traditional, modern; they are all different expressions of the family of God. Find a Church that suits you and feels like home. A Church where: Jesus is glorified, the Bible is taught, people are helped to become more like Jesus, and the environment is loving and accepting. Just remember too, that there is no such thing as a perfect Church, because Churches are made up of imperfect sheep, who are on a journey with their shepherd, just like you. As Billy Graham said, "If you find a perfect Church, don't join it, you'll spoil it." (6)

Now in Psalm 23 the Hebrew word used for "want" in "I shall not be in want" makes it clear what kind of want it is talking about, because the word means to lack or to need (7), so David is talking about the second type of want, lacking a necessity of life. He is saying, "With the Lord as my shepherd, what more do I need?" He is declaring, "With the Lord as my shepherd, I know I will have everything I need for a complete and full life." Did not Jesus say:

> I have come that they may have life, and have it to the full. (John 10:10).

MEETING OUR EVERY NEED

David now paints a picture for us of some of the ways in which the Lord meets our every need.

First of all, "He makes me lie down in green pastures." Now if you are a sheep, to be presented with green pasture means you've hit the jackpot. Green grass is tender and succulent, it's nutritious and fresh. If you were a sheep your mouth would be watering right now. And if you were a sheep in the Middle East you might be particularly excited, because in a dry and hot land finding green pasture is not that easy. Grass can quickly become brown and dry and tough. Have you ever eaten a steak like that?

But there's something else here too, because the word for pasture, as well as meaning pasture, also means habitation, house or pleasant place (8). The Lord my shepherd wants me to be in a pleasant place. I love that thought. And there is a sense of rest here, because it says "He makes me lie down". To lie down means to rest. And to lie down for a sheep is particularly significant, because a sheep will only lie down if it feels completely safe.

> *Making It Real:*
> *So here's another question for you – how safe do you feel? Are you standing like a meerkat, or lying down like a sheep who feels safe in the care of its shepherd? If you don't feel safe and secure right now, then talk to your heavenly Father about it, because he wants to give you rest in a pleasant place. No matter what is going on around us, there is no heavenly reason why, in our soul, we can't be lying down in green pastures.*

Then in the next line we read, "He leads me beside quiet waters." Here David continues and reinforces the theme of rest. There is a strong repetition going on here, because the word to lead means to lead or guide to a watering place, bring to a place of rest, to refresh (9). And the word for quiet, or still in some translations, means resting place or rest (10). So David is saying here, "The Lord my shepherd guides me to a place of rest, to a place of refreshing". Now, from what I've read about sheep, they can only drink from quiet or still water. If necessary, shepherds would create a dam in a flowing stream to make a pool of water for the sheep to drink from. So the message seems very clear here, God knows that I need a place of rest and refreshment where I can feel safe and secure, and my Good Shepherd supplies it to me for a specific reason – because, "He restores my soul".

RESTORATION AND REST

God is in the restoration business, he wants to restore you, he wants to restore me. When David talks about "my soul", he is talking about that part of you that is your inner being, your life, your desires, your passions, your emotions, what makes you, you. He is talking about your inner world that only you and God see. The rest of us only see the results of your inner world. As Jesus said:

A good man brings good things out of the good stored up in him, and an evil man brings evil things out of the evil stored up in him. (Matthew 12:35)

So why do our souls need restoring? Well there can be many reasons. For a start, life is not all about lying down in green pastures. Life can be tough; the way can be hard. Ships are not made for remaining in harbour they are made for the high seas, they are made to weather the storm, but they do need to return to harbour frequently. Sheep need to keep moving, if they just stayed in one place all the time, they would quickly run out of grass to eat, but they also need regular times of safe rest too. Following Christ and serving God can drain us, we have an enemy who can deceive and attack us, we live in a fallen world that can torment us, and we have a sinful nature that can trip us up. In John 16:33 Jesus said:

> In this world you will have trouble. But take heart! I have overcome the world.

Jesus has defeated our enemy and overcome the world, and we can overcome whatever life throws at us, in part, because the Lord restores our soul. From Psalm 23 we see that rest is an important part of that restoration process, indeed in the Old Testament to take a Sabbath rest was a command from God. Now our 24/7 society makes it hard to find an hour, let alone a whole day of rest. Our society tends to idolise busyness, we can wear our busy schedule as a badge of honour, because we think that if we are busy then we must be being successful. We have the saying "work hard and play hard", and there is nothing wrong with that, but our souls need more. We confuse leisure with rest. We have never had so much leisure time, we even have a leisure industry eager to help us spend our leisure time, and yet at the same time being 'Tired All The Time' (TATT) is now such a common reason for visits to the doctor that it has its own acronym.

The kind of Sabbath rest that our shepherd has designed for us, to restore our souls, is quite different from what we think of as leisure.

William Wilberforce was a Christian Member of Parliament (MP), who 200 years ago caused Parliament to outlaw slavery throughout the British Empire. It took nearly 20 years of battling against vested interests and big business to achieve his goal and it is seen as one of the greatest and most courageous acts of statesmanship in the history of democracy (11). But it wouldn't have happened without William Wilberforce's habit of Sabbath rest. There was a point in his political career when he was in the running for a cabinet post. One of his biographers writes:

> It did not take long for Wilberforce to become preoccupied with the possibility of the appointment. For days it grabbed at his conscious mind, forcing aside everything else. By his own admission he had the "rising of ambition, and it was crippling his soul." (Garth Lean) But Sunday brought the cure. In his diary Wilberforce says, "Blessed be to God for the day of rest and religious occupation wherein earthly things assume their true size. Ambition is stunted. (11)

Wilberforce had discovered that the person who establishes a block of time for Sabbath rest on a regular basis is able to keep life in a proper perspective, avoid burnout and maintain a clear vision of God's purpose.

Making It Real:
So how is it with your soul?
Does your inner world feel in need of some restoration?
Do you need to let your shepherd restore your soul?
Then make a decision to establish a regular rhythm of rest in your life, a time of solitude and

> *quiet with God. Read his word, listen for his voice, give him time to restore your soul. Do it daily, do it weekly in a Sabbath rest. Remember this is God's design, HE is the one who leads you beside still waters, HE is the one who MAKES you lie down in green pastures. Don't let the busyness of the world rob you of your shepherd's gift of rest; allow him to do his restoring work in your inner world.*

About one hundred and fifty years ago a Christian called Horatio Spafford wrote a hymn. He was a wealthy man with a thriving legal practice in Chicago, a beautiful home, a wife, four daughters and a son. Then he suffered the tragic loss of his son, followed shortly after by the Great Chicago fire that destroyed almost every investment that he had made. He sent his wife and daughters to England for a much-needed holiday, only to later receive a letter saying that his four daughters had drowned in a collision at sea, only his wife survived. Most of us cannot begin to imagine the pain and grief that he suffered. On his voyage to England to comfort his grieving wife he had time to sit and rest at the feet of his shepherd. During the voyage he wrote the hymn "It is well with my Soul". The first verse says:

> When peace, like a river, attendeth my way,
> When sorrows like sea billows roll;
> Whatever my lot, Thou hast taught me to say,
> It is well, it is well with my soul. (12)

These are the words of a man who does not want, who has found all the strength he needs in Christ his saviour, and whose soul is being restored as he allows his shepherd to make him lie down in green pastures.

You and I have the same great shepherd, who knows and understands the circumstances of our lives. What more do we need?

3. HE GUIDES ME

He guides me in paths of righteousness for his name's sake. (Psalm 23:3)

How are you when it comes to making decisions? Do you make them quickly, confident in the right path to take, or do decisions stress you out for fear of making a mistake? Well I'm definitely towards the stressed-out end of the spectrum. It's not that I can't make decisions, I do it all the time, I can even make decisions quickly when I'm on familiar ground, but I know that if I had the choice, I'd sooner put a decision off, and do some more research and analysis, rather than actually decide.

What I find so hard about making a decision is that there seems no place to hide. I have to make it, it's down to me, and my thinking becomes focused on me. Have I considered all the options? Have I heard God properly? Am I open to what God wants? But thanks to Psalm 23, I've realised quite recently that it doesn't have to be like that. Psalm 23:3 says:

He guides me in paths of righteousness for his name's sake.

One of the wonderful things about Psalm 23, is that it doesn't focus on what I need to do, it concentrates on what God does, and the language is all in the present moment: The Lord is my shepherd; He makes me lie down; He leads me; He restores my soul. These things are wonderful and amazing enough, and we looked at them already, but in a way they lay the foundation for what comes next, "He guides me". He, the Lord, the maker of Heaven and Earth, my saviour who is my shepherd guides me. Every time I think of this, I can feel the stress of decision-making melting away.

THE GUIDE WHO DOES NOT HIDE

What can add to the stress of making a decision, of finding God's will, is a feeling deep down, perhaps unacknowledged, and probably unsaid, that God's will is somehow hidden from us, and it is our job to find it. Like an egg hunt, but less fun. Well, there will be some seeking involved. To seek is a good thing; seeking develops our heart and soul. The Bible tells us to seek the Lord: his face; his council; his will. He promises that if we seek him, we will find him. Our seeking can be in confidence and peace, because Psalm 23 tells us that he is the guide who does not hide. Our shepherd guides us to the right path, he does not hide it from us. If we can really grasp this, if we really take it to heart, what a difference this can make to the way we see decision making. Dictionary.com defines "guide" as, "to assist a person to travel through… an unfamiliar area." (13) Do you feel like you're travelling through unfamiliar territory? Do not be afraid, your shepherd is guiding you.

Now there are two types of guide, one gives directions, and the other accompanies the person being guided. So what kind of guide do we have in the Lord? Does he accompany us through the unfamiliar territory, or does he give us directions? Psalm 23 makes it very clear. Does a shepherd gather his sheep together and say, "Now then sheep, there is this wonderful green pasture I've got ready for you. All you need to do is follow this path, turn left at the big rock and then turn right at the river. You can't miss it. I'll be waiting for you there." No, he doesn't say that. Shepherds are with their sheep every step of the way, they lead them. Actually, the shepherd's presence, the fact that they can see him, is their guide. Has not God said,

'Never will I leave you; never will I forsake you' (Hebrews 13:5).

Making It Real:
Are you facing a big decision right now, are you wanting to know God's will? If you are, then take your stress levels way down by remembering that the Lord is your shepherd and he is guiding you. There's another really comforting thing here about the way God guides us. If God guides

> *you only by giving you instructions, then if you do take a wrong turn, you're lost. If you turn right at the big rock instead of left, then you will never come to the river, so the instructions would become useless. They would be as useful as when you ask someone for directions and they say, "Well I wouldn't start from here." But if your guide is with you, as our shepherd has promised to be with us, then if you do make a wrong turn, he will adjust his guidance to get you to the right place. So if, like me, you're stressed by the thought of making the wrong choice, then take comfort from the fact that your guide is always with you. He will guide you from where you are, wherever that might be.*

IN WHAT DIRECTION?

So the next question is, in what direction is he guiding me? The answer is:

...in paths of righteousness...

But what does that mean? Well first of all, what is a path? A path is a means to get somewhere. If you're on a path you don't say, "Great I've arrived, I'm on a path." If he guides me in paths, it means that his guidance is about the journey, not the destination. Some people say, "The end justifies the means", but our shepherd's guidance is about the means not the end. Those who trust in Jesus have a sure destination, which is why Jesus said:

My Father's house has many rooms; if that were not so, would I have told you that I am going there to prepare a place for you? And if I go and prepare a place for you, I will come back and take you to be with me that you also may be where I am. (John 14:2-3)

Jesus is coming back for us, to take us to be with him. We can be confident of our final destination. So our life now is really all about the journey. Hebrews 11:9 says about Abraham that:

By faith he made his home in the promised land like a stranger in a foreign country; he lived in tents.

In the same way, it is good for us to remember that we are just passing through, what we have now is only temporary accommodation. Our home is in heaven. Let's not get too attached to anything on earth. As the apostle Paul says:

So we fix our eyes not on what is seen, but on what is unseen, since what is seen is temporary, but what is unseen is eternal. (2 Corinthians 4:18)

We cannot go on a journey without leaving some things behind, and so it is with our spiritual journey. We cannot take hold of all that our shepherd loving has for us, if we are holding on too tightly to what we have. The writer to the Hebrews goes on to say:

…let us throw off everything that hinders and the sin that so easily entangles. And let us run with perseverance the race marked out for us, fixing our eyes on Jesus, the pioneer and perfecter of faith. (Hebrews 12:1,2)

What this means in practice is holding everything in an open hand to God, whilst keeping our eyes fixed on our shepherd as he leads the way.

Making It Real:
Is there anything in your life that you are holding onto too tightly?
Do you need to look into your good shepherd's face and open your hand?

So it's about the journey, a journey taken with our shepherd, and we need his guidance because there are multiple paths. It says "He guides me in PATHS". Have you ever wondered why it says paths, and not path? Here is my thought: as we travel through the Christian life, from time to time, there will be a change of direction required, a new path to follow. There was not necessarily anything wrong with the old path, but now God guides us onto a new path. In fact there is a principle in the way God guides us which is this, "No news is good news". Isaiah 30:21 says:

Whether you turn to the right or to the left, your ears will hear a voice behind you, saying, 'This is the way; walk in it.'

Your Sat Nav does not say to you every 5 minutes, "stay on this road, stay on this road". I suspect that would get rather irritating. Your Sat Nav gives you directions just before you need to turn onto a new road. So it is with God. When we need to take a new path, we will hear his voice behind us saying 'This is the way; walk in it.'

Toward the end of my full-time working life, I felt as if I was hearing his voice. I'd worked for Rolls-Royce for thirty-eight years, as a Mechanical Engineer and Manager. I'd really enjoyed my job, God had blessed me through it, and he had taught me something of what it means to work to please him and not to please other people. But then I started to consider early retirement. Up until twelve months before, I could never understand why anyone would want to take early retirement. But God changed my view of it completely. It seemed that there was now a different voice calling me. There was a lot more seeking God, and because it was me, a lot more thinking and analysing to do (remember fast decisions are not my strong point), but what I found so wonderful about our shepherd is that he knows our strengths and weaknesses and guides us accordingly. He knew how slow I am so he slowly changed my thinking and feelings on the subject. Six months after teaching on this very subject, I had left Rolls-Royce after thirty-nine years, and my stress levels were far lower, through the whole thing, thanks to the revelation that my shepherd was guiding me.

PATHS OF RIGHTEOUSNESS?

So, he guides me in paths, but in what kind of paths? In "paths of righteousness". Righteousness isn't a word we use very often, so its meaning can be a little fuzzy. Righteousness can be defined as "behaviour that is morally right" (14). A righteous act is the morally right thing to do. Righteousness is one of the foundations of our Lord's character:

Righteousness and justice are the foundation of your throne; love and faithfulness go before you. (Psalm 89:14)

I love that picture of God's power and authority being built on righteousness and justice. It is impossible for God to do the wrong thing. The apostle John puts it like this:

God is light; in him there is no darkness at all (1 John 1:5).

The wonderful thing about our Shepherd is that love and faithfulness go before him. If we ask for forgiveness, he will give it freely:

If we claim to be without sin, we deceive ourselves and the truth is not in us. If we confess our sins, he is faithful and just and will forgive us our sins and purify us from all unrighteousness. (1 John 1:8,9)

Even as Christians who trust in Jesus, we are not perfect. As sheep, we continue to wander from the righteous path. When we confess our sins to God, his righteousness says, "Your sin needs punishment", but in his faithfulness God remembers that Jesus has paid for your sin on the Cross. So then his justice says, "Because Jesus has PAID the penalty for your sin, I will cleanse you from it completely, I will make you as white as snow". In this way, God's righteousness and justice are satisfied completely, and he sees us as if we had never sinned. This amazing gift of forgiveness is possible because God's love went before him, and moved him to provide such a great salvation.

Hallelujah, what a saviour! Does your heart leap for joy at the wonder of his grace? The majesty of it hit me in a fresh way through this picture of God's character, in the way that his righteousness and his justice and his love and his faithfulness work together to reveal the glory of his amazing grace.

It is as if they form the four corners of an enormous banner that declares the wonder and glory of God's grace to all of heaven and earth for all eternity. They form a glorious tension, because the greater his righteousness, the greater his love must be that desires to save us. And the greater his Justice, the greater his faithfulness must be in forgiving us. Is it any wonder that we sing "Amazing Grace"?

So we are no longer condemned by our lack of righteousness, but we are called to make righteousness our aim. When we do the right thing, we walk with God, because:

Righteousness goes before him and prepares the way for his steps. (Psalm 85:13)

Making It Real:
Righteousness goes before God like a red carpet, and so our shepherd will only take righteous steps. That means that he will only guide us in righteousness paths. So here is an application

for us. When we are facing a decision, it is good to ask ourselves this question – What is the righteous path?

Not all decisions have a moral dimension, but many do. If the path you are contemplating involves any deception, any immorality, any exploitation or harm to others, then it is not a righteous path, and your shepherd will not be guiding you there. But sometimes we can face really difficult choices where there seems no way out, "stuck between a rock and a hard place". But our shepherd always provides a way out, and that way will be a righteous path based on truth, integrity and humility. It's about the journey, remember, not the destination. How we do things matters just as much as what we do. There's a saying, that I heard a long-time ago, "Satan rushes people - God guides them" (source unknown). God will not rush you down a righteous path.

FOR HIS NAME'S SAKE?

Here then is the motivation for it all. Why does our shepherd guide us in paths of righteousness? "...for his name's sake." Now in the Bible names carry great significance, because someone's name defines who they are: their character; their authority; their reputation; their honour. So, it is for the sake of his character, including his righteousness, justice, love and faithfulness that our shepherd will guide us. It is for the sake of his authority, his reputation and even his honour that he guides us in paths of righteousness.

Making It Real:
This brings us to one of the deepest truths in all scripture:
It is not about you; it is all about him.
This truth will set you free.
About the eternal God, God the Son, Jesus Christ – Colossians 1:16 tells us that, "all things were made by him and for him", and that includes you and me. You and I exist for our Lord Jesus, to live for him, and he enables us to do that by being our shepherd. If we miss or forget this truth, then we not only miss the purpose of our very existence, we also inevitably damage our life in time and eternity.
Is your aim in life to live by him and for him?

Has our shepherd not demonstrated to us that we can trust him with our very life? Are paths of righteousness always easy? No, sometimes they are hard, but they will always bring glory to God, they will always please him, and that is their purpose.

The Lord is your shepherd, and he is committed to guide you for his glory. His righteousness and justice will ensure that your path is righteous; his love will ensure that your path will be for your good, and his faithfulness will mean that he will always be with you on your path. Jesus walks before you as your shepherd guiding you, while the Holy Spirit walks behind you shining his light over your shoulder so that you can see Jesus. At the same time the Spirit whispers in your ear, "This is the path", as he lights up God's word to instruct and feed you.

I don't want to give the impression that guidance is easy, there are two factors that can make it complicated. First of all, we always have a choice. We have the freedom to not follow our Shepherd's guidance. Self-will, stubbornness, sin, whatever you want to call it, can make us deaf to our shepherd's guidance. This is why 90% of knowing God's will is being prepared to do it, whatever it might be. And secondly, we have an enemy that wants to distract us and misdirect us, with temptations and lies. I think that David Gooding's encouragement has the answer to this problem:

He requires us to test everything that claims to be the Holy Spirit's guidance by this basic principle: nothing that the Holy Spirit leads us to do will ever go contrary to the character and teaching of the Lord Jesus. (15)

This is what it means to be led in paths of righteousness for his name's sake.

> *Making It Real:*
> *So, trust in the Lord, rest in his promise to guide you. Wait for him, listen for his voice. Read his word, talk to other Christians. Be open, because righteous paths are not secretive, they are well lit.*

Proverbs 4:18 says:

The path of the righteous is like the morning sun, shining ever brighter till the full light of day.

He is guiding you on a path that is glorious. He is guiding you on the path to glory.

4. WALK THROUGH THE VALLEY

Even though I walk through the valley
of the shadow of death,
I will fear no evil,
for you are with me;
your rod and your staff,
they comfort me. (Psalm 23:4)

Our environment affects how we feel. There is a whole body of research around this that shows even colours affect our mood. Apparently blues de-stress us and even decrease our blood pressure, while yellows inspire happiness. So far, our journey through Psalm 23 has painted a picture of abundant ease, lived in a pleasant environment of green pastures and quiet waters. But now we are heading for a change of scenery, the valley awaits us. Verse 4 says this:

Even though I walk through the valley
of the shadow of death,
I will fear no evil,
for you are with me;
your rod and your staff,
they comfort me.

As a shepherd boy, David would have been very familiar with the need to travel through harsh environments to get from one feeding ground to another. At times the sheep would have to pass through deep, rugged valleys called wadis. The air in the bottom of these wadis gets heavy, hot and oppressive. These narrow gorges can feel very far indeed from the open, green pastures where the sheep lay down to rest. These wadis are full of deep, dark shadows, where anything could be lying in wait. As a sheep, whose instinct is to flee from danger, you would feel trapped and hemmed in, with nowhere to run. In cowboy films, the ambush always happens in a deep valley like this. David called it the valley of the shadow of death, or the darkest valley. The word used for shadow here carries the meaning of deep darkness, extreme danger or distress (16).

Making It Real:
We all pass through a dark valley at some point, perhaps you are in a dark valley right now, perhaps there is even the shadow of death in your valley for you or a loved one. Do you feel hemmed in, on a path that you want to run away from, but can't? Facing facts that we would

> *rather avoid, as Abraham once did (Romans 4:19), does not weaken our faith, but strengthens it. Do you have someone you can confide in? It helps to express the truth about how we feel to another human being as well as our shepherd.*

One of the darkest valleys I have been through was when our daughter became ill. As her parents, for a time we didn't know what to do. For me there were two key things that became clear. First, I had to hold on to a lifeline that God put in my heart. It was a scripture which just seemed to express the confidence I wanted to have in God, in the midst of bewilderment, uncertainty and chaos. The scripture was Romans 10:13:

Everyone who calls on the name of the Lord will be saved.

I didn't know what was happening to my lovely daughter, I didn't know what the future would hold for her or for us, but this I did know – If I called to the Lord for help, he would save us. I knew I could trust in him. In those dark days God pulled out of me a confidence and hope in him that I did not know I had. I am eternally grateful to him for that.

The second thing that became clear was that I needed to accept that our daughter might never be able to go to university. In my job I worked with Professors, I had to admit that academic achievement was important to me, and I was proud of what both our children had achieved at school. But I had to lay all that on the altar before God. Part of my trusting in him was to let go of what I had hoped for, and put my hope in him, trusting that in his love and faithfulness a different future, if that was his will, would be for our good.

In the winter of 2007, we walked through a very dark valley, but we never felt alone, our shepherd was with us, he comforted and helped us. Then our daughter did start to recover, she gradually returned to school, completed her exams, got her grades and went to her chosen university. It was a miracle that had seemed impossible to us in the dark days of that winter. Less than a year later, she was able to write this:

> After the summer I found out that I had the grades I needed to go to my first choice of university. I am now having the best time of my life there and I know it is all down to God. Looking back on those months in the beginning of 2007 I realise that, even though it didn't feel like it at the time, God was with me all the way. He was looking after me and had a plan for me, and I now feel so much closer to him, stronger and more confident in him because of that time of my life. Praise God.

Praise God indeed!

WALK THROUGH!

So if that was my experience of walking through a dark valley, what was King David's experience? Well, first of all, he makes a very simple but profound point, because he starts by saying, "Even though I WALK through the valley." There may not be a way OUT of the valley, but there is a way THROUGH - keep walking.

> *Making It Real:*
> *When we are in a dark place, the one thing we should not do is lie down. Our shepherd wants us to lie down and rest in green pastures, not in dark valleys. If we lie down in a dark place, through exhaustion, self-pity or any other reason, nothing will change. But if we keep walking, eventually we will come through it, we will come out into the green pastures our shepherd has for us. It is true what people say about the hard times of life, "Take it one day at a time." Take it one step at a time.*

NO EVIL?

Then David declares something quite remarkable, "I will fear no evil". I will fear NO evil! The word evil here means: adversity, affliction, calamity or distress (17). So David is saying, "Even though I am going through a time of great uncertainty, pain, loss and even death, I will not fear what might happen to me." How amazing is that? Fear would be a very natural response to such an environment. Like a sheep, our biology is designed to equip us to run from danger, propelled by the adrenaline released by fear. We might be subject to our biology, but our theology enables us to have a different response. How can our theology override our biology? David gives us the answer - by faith. He declares, "For YOU are with me". And by faith we can be certain that the Lord, the Lion of Judah, the almighty God, creator of all things, our shepherd, is with US too. Faith like this is the antidote to fear.

Time and time again in his life David came back to this fundamental truth. In Psalm 27:1 he says:

> The Lord is my light and my salvation –
>   whom shall I fear?
> The Lord is the stronghold of my life –
>   of whom shall I be afraid?

FREE FROM FEAR

> *Making It Real:*
> *Our shepherd intends that we experience his love every day, by living a life that is FREE FROM FEAR ...even in the darkest times. Is that your experience?*

Psalm 112:6-8 says this:

Surely the righteous will never be shaken...
They will have no fear of bad news;
their hearts are steadfast, trusting in the Lord.
Their hearts are secure, they will have no fear.

We are living in a fear epidemic, stoked in part by a 24/7 media that makes tragedies from around the world seem part of our everyday experience, or makes a global pandemic appear to be crouching at our door. We live in a time of great uncertainty, when important things that we once thought we could rely upon, like a job for life, have been taken from us. Perhaps not since World War II has a generation been exposed to such uncertainty and fear. The causes may be different, but the effects can be the same. In such a time as this, if you want to live your life free from fear then remind yourself, every day, that your shepherd is with you, every step of the way. Trust in him, your shepherd is with you always, and he is mighty to save.

My wife has struggled with fear and anxiety all her life, and one of the things that has helped her is to, from time to time, raise up an Ebenezer. The word Ebenezer "comes from a Hebrew phrase that means 'stone of help.' The name appears in the Biblical story told in the Book of 1 Samuel, in which the Hebrew prophet Samuel sets up a stone to commemorate the help that God had given the Israelites." (18)

Then Samuel took a stone and set it up between Mizpah and Shen. He named it Ebenezer, saying, 'Thus far the Lord has helped us.' (1 Samuel 7:12)

Making It Real:
When you experience your shepherd's help in a significant way, let me encourage you to raise up an Ebenezer to declare to yourself then, but also to remind yourself in the future, what God has done. Commemorate God's goodness in some way: place a stone in your garden, or in your pocket as my wife does; write it in your journal; tell others. Raise up your Ebenezers, and your fears will go down.

YOUR ROD AND STAFF

David then goes on to say, "Your rod and your staff, they comfort me". Now I don't know about you, but the thought of a rod and staff do not immediately fill me with comfort. Right from childhood I've imagined that they were perhaps intended to hit me on the head when I stepped out of line. But thankfully, that is not the meaning here at all. The rod and staff were tools of the trade for a shepherd. The rod was the tool he used to defend his sheep, but also to gather his sheep together, and to count them. Ezekiel 20:37 says:

> I will take note of you as you pass under my rod, and I will bring you into the bond of the covenant.

I love that, "I will take note of you..." What a comfort it is to know that God does not just see us as one of a flock, he takes note of us as individuals. When a sheep passed under the shepherd's rod, his focus was on that sheep, and that sheep alone. The wonderful thing about our good shepherd, and our Heavenly Father, is that in his eyes we are always under his rod, he is always taking note of us.

The staff was the shepherd's walking stick, and the word can mean support of any kind (19). If a sheep gets stuck or trapped, the shepherd can use his staff to give them the help that they need.

I've been close to serious injury or death twice in my life, as far as I know. I was once helping with some building work, and as I climbed down a ladder onto a roof, the ladder slipped. I found myself holding on to the ladder as the ladder and I slid down into an awaiting skip full of all kinds of debris. My life did not flash before my eyes, but time did seem to stand still. I was not afraid, but I'm not very quick thinking in situations like this. I just remember thinking something like, "This will be interesting". The next thing I knew, I was lying on the roof wrapped in someone's arms. Unbeknown to me, my friend, who used to be a fireman, was standing on the roof below me, and as I slid past him, he snatched me from the ladder by wrapping his arms around me. I thank God for his strength, quick thinking and skill, and for placing him in the right place at the right time. It felt like God used him as a human staff of the shepherd that day. He pulled me out of harm's way.

The other life threating occasion occurred during a race in a small sailing boat. I was crewing, well I was ballast really. We were tacking in high wind, and as we changed direction we capsized. Being new to sailing I didn't really know what to do, and as I have already said, I'm rather slow-thinking in situations like this, so I just observed the boat start to roll over. Again, time seemed to slow down, and at some point, I realised that I was going to finish up underneath an overturned hull. "Well", I thought, "There'll be an air pocket underneath the boat, so I should be fine". But as I tried to position myself to make use of the air pocket, I realised that my lifejacket was caught on something behind me. I kept trying to move, but just couldn't. Was I going to finish up trapped upside-down, in an upside-down boat? There was no fear, it all happened too quickly for fear, but I do remember thinking, "This will be interesting, what if I can't breathe?" Then suddenly my lifejacket became free, and I was able to move into the air pocket. It was as if my shepherd unhooked me with his staff, without the help of human hands this time. How grateful I am for my shepherd's staff.

I'm grateful too for the skipper, who realising that he couldn't see me, looked under the water, saw my legs under the boat, dived down, grabbed my leg and pulled me from underneath the boat. All this, by the way, was caught on video by a camera that was attached to the rigging.

Making It Real:
Are you comforted to know that when the going gets tough, and you find yourself in a precarious or dangerous situation, your shepherd is there equipped to help you? Are you trapped by something? Do you need your shepherd to set you free with his staff? Very often his staff will take the form of a person, someone who cares for you. Do you need to ask a trusted person for help? Perhaps you need help to walk through the valley. Then know this, the shepherd of your soul takes note of you, he has his eye upon you, and his help is at hand. Ask for his help. Look for his help. He has promised to care for you.

HOW TO STRENGTHEN YOUR FAITH

So even though we walk through the valley of the shadow of death, we will fear no evil, for our shepherd is with us. But sometimes trusting in God does not come easily to us; sometimes we struggle to live a life free from fear.

> *Making It Real:*
> *Do you want to trust your shepherd more? Here are seven things that we can do to strengthen our faith and help us live a life free from fear:*
> *1) Call on the name of the Lord.*
> *2) Listen to God*
> *3) Present your requests to God*
> *4) Remember what he has done*
> *5) Lay down your plans and wait for his plan to unfold*
> *6) Keep walking*
> *7) You'll never walk alone*

Here are the seven faith strengtheners in more detail:

1) Call on the name of the Lord.

This is what I discovered to be my life-line. When we call on his name, we are declaring our trust in his character and his promises; we are declaring our dependence on him and him alone, to save us. There is no valley too deep, no valley too dark, for his love to reach us.

2)   Listen to God.
Romans 10:17 says:

So then faith comes by hearing, and hearing by the word of God.

Hearing the word of God causes faith to grow. But in order to hear we must listen. Have you ever considered how amazing it is that God Almighty, the creator of heaven and earth, wants to speak to you? He has a whole universe to run! And yet the Bible tells us clearly that God does desire to speak to us. The question is do we take the time to listen? God does not shout. As Elijah discovered in 1 Kings 19, the Lord does not come in a powerful wind, an earthquake, or a fire. No, The Lord comes in a gentle whisper. To listen to God, we need to find a quiet place.

It is when we hear the word of God that faith comes, and God speaks first and foremost through his written word the Bible, as we read it, study it or hear it spoken. It is through the Bible that God speaks to us, because the Holy Spirit takes the things of God and makes them real to us. So, if you want your faith to grow – listen to Bible based teaching and preaching, and most important of all, make time, and find a quiet place, to read the Bible for yourself, asking God to speak to your heart and mind and soul. I think that our experience teaches all of us that making time is one of the hardest parts of this. Unless we set aside time, unless we protect time, unless we make time to be still and focus on the word of God, then we will not hear from God. Making time is our part in this, speaking truth and life to our souls is the Holy Spirit's part.

As we listen, we will also know better how to pray, which brings us to...

3)   Present your requests to God.
Philippians 4:6 says:

Do not be anxious about anything, but in every situation, by prayer and petition, with thanksgiving, present your requests to God.

It says, "In EVERY situation" - there is no valley too deep or dark from which the Lord your God does not want to hear your requests. And the promise from verse 7 that goes along with this is:

And the peace of God, which transcends all understanding, will guard your hearts and your minds in Christ Jesus.

Our shepherd does not promise to remove us immediately from our dark valley, but he does promise us peace, peace that can defy logic and understanding. Such peace comes as we make our requests to our shepherd.

4)   Remember what he has done.
About the children of Israel when they were too afraid to enter the promised land Psalm 106:13 says this:

But they soon forgot what he had done and did not wait for his plan to unfold.

Time and time again the Bible encourages us to remember what God has done for us. Why? Because it feeds our faith. Israel could have remembered how God had parted the Red sea and defeated all of Pharaoh's army without them lifting a finger, and said, "Well if God did that for us then, he can do it again". But they didn't. They allowed fear to rule them, and they missed out on God's blessing as a result. So take time to think back over your life, and all the ways that your shepherd has helped you, guided you, cared for you, provided for you, and yes, saved you. And then…

5)   Lay down your own plans and wait for his plan to unfold.

When the way is hard and dark, holding on to your own hopes and plans just weighs you down. It can be a great burden lifted, and a source of freedom, when we lay our plans at his feet, and say, "Not my will, but yours be done". Make your plans the subject of your requests to God, yes, but hold them in an open hand before him.

Psalm 106:13 also says they "did not wait for his plan to unfold". The thing about a dark valley is that you can't see the way ahead. You don't know what is around the next corner, or in the dark shadow. But you can know that your shepherd is with you, and that he has a plan for you, a plan to prosper you and not to harm you. A plan to give you a hope and a future (Jeremiah 29:11). You can trust that his plan will become clear, you just need to wait for it to unfold. You need to be patient, and as you wait for his plan to unfold, you also need to:

6)   Keep walking.

Waiting for his plans to unfold is not a passive activity. We need to keep walking, keep following our shepherd, doing what we know he wants us to do. Get on with life as best as you can.

And then finally, if you are only going to take one thing away from Psalm 23:4, let it be this:

7)   You'll never walk alone.

What Psalm 23:4 teaches us more than anything else is that as a Christian our identity is defined by "YOU ARE WITH ME". It is a foundation of who you are in Christ to know that "you'll never walk alone".

Of course, "You'll never walk alone" (20) is a famous song. It was written by Rodgers and Hammerstein in 1945 for their musical "Carousel". It was sung to comfort a grieving widow. In 1963 Gerry and the Pacemakers released a version that got to Number One, and it was adopted by Liverpool Football Club as their anthem not long after that.

This song is very moving for me, because it has connections to my parents, who were both in amateur dramatics. When I was about twelve, all three of us took part in the musical Carousel together. This song stirs something deep within all of us that longs to know that we are not alone. But the song also leaves an important question unanswered – Who will walk with us? Part of the song's appeal is that it leaves it up to us to answer that question. Football fans sing "You'll Never Walk Alone" to their players to tell them that they will support them no matter what. How must the team feel when they hear 20,000 supporters singing this to them? Whatever hidden strength it causes to well up within them, I want to tell you, it is nothing compared to what we have, because Almighty God, the creator of all things, is the one singing it to you. Zephaniah 3:17 says this:

'The Lord your God is with you, the Mighty Warrior who saves. He will take great delight in you; in his love he will no longer rebuke you, but will rejoice over you with singing.'

He will rejoice over you with singing!

As you walk through the valley of the shadow of death your shepherd is singing to you saying, "Fear not for I am with you. You'll never walk alone."

5. MY CUP OVERFLOWS

You prepare a table before me
in the presence of my enemies.
You anoint my head with oil;
my cup overflows. (Psalm 23:5)

Do you have any pet hates? One of mine is when a restaurant gives me a cup of tea that is only half full. Quite apart from the thermodynamics of it (sorry that's engineer speak for a lot of cup and not much hot water = lukewarm tea), there's also the loss of potential. There's all that space in the top of the cup going to waste. Someone put that space there to be used for containing tea, why not use it? And apart from anything else it just seems mean.

Why am I telling you this? Because we now move into the part of Psalm 23 that is the opposite of my pet hate. So far in our walk through Psalm 23, the picture has been very clearly around shepherds and sheep, where the Lord our God is the shepherd and we are his sheep. Some people believe that all of Psalm 23 is about shepherds and sheep, but I find myself agreeing with those who see

David as changing his perspective in the latter part of his Psalm. For one thing scripture talks elsewhere of anointing the heads of people with oil, but not sheep. So it seems to me that in verse 5, the shepherd boy, who became King, starts to paint a different picture of his experience of God, where the Lord is the generous host and we are his guests. He says:

You prepare a table before me
    in the presence of my enemies.
You anoint my head with oil;
    my cup overflows.
    (Psalm 23:5)

YOU PREPARE A TABLE FOR ME?

So David starts his picture of the Lord as his generous host by saying, "You prepare a table before me." I love the way David speaks directly to God here. He says YOU prepare…, and it made me ask myself the question, "How often do I say directly to God, 'YOU have done this for me', in a very personal and direct way?" Not often enough. So if you are like me, let's aim to include more, "You… for me" statements of gratitude and trust in our relationship with God like:

Thank you, Lord, that you provided for me today.
Thank you, Lord, that you protected me today.
Thank you, Lord, that you gave me wisdom today.

So the focus here is on what God does for you, what God does for me. What does he do? He prepares a table before YOU. What, before me? Yes, before YOU. Now that word, "prepare", here means to set in a row, to arrange, to put in order (21). This tells us something important about God our generous host, it tells us that he likes order, and that he works to create order in our lives. In the context of worship, 1 Corinthians 14:33 in the Amplified Bible says:

for God ... is not a God of confusion and disorder but of peace and order.

And consequently, in verse 40 it says:

But everything should be done in a fitting and orderly way.

So God is not a God of confusion, he creates order. This made me wonder, if we want to know how much we weigh we get on a weighing-scale, so if we want to know how ordered our lives are, can we use an "Order Scale"? Therefore I've produced this:

The Order Scale

10 — Perfect peace. My life is arranged in line with God's purpose for my life.

9

8

7

6

5

4

3

2

1 — Completely lost. My life is falling apart. I don't know if I'm coming or going.

Making It Real:

Where is your life right now, on the Order Scale? Are you feeling in perfect peace, with your life arranged and ordered in line with God's purpose for your life? Or are you at the other end of the scale feeling completely lost in chaos, like your life is falling apart, not knowing if you are coming or going? More likely you are feeling somewhere in between the two. Where we feel we are on the order scale can change with our circumstances. If we are walking through a dark valley, we would probably move down, and if we're lying down in green pastures, we'll probably move up, but the message for us here, is that wherever we are, God wants to take us up the Order Scale.

BUILDING PEACE AND ORDER

So how does God build order in our lives? Well he builds it from the bottom up, he builds it from a firm foundation. The only foundation that brings true order to our lives is Jesus Christ. Giving our life to Jesus, asking for and receiving his forgiveness is the beginning of true order. From that point God becomes our Heavenly Father, and he also becomes our generous host who arranges a table of delights for us. He gives us the Holy Spirit to be our Wonderful Counsellor, and he sets us free with the truth. Truth may be painful, but in the end, truth brings order and peace. Truth comes through knowledge, and true knowledge comes through revelation. One of the truths that is essential to a life of peace and order in Christ is contained in one of my favourite verses in the whole Bible:

I write these things to you who believe in the name of the Son of God so that you may know that you have eternal life. (1 John 5:13)

I love that – "so that you may KNOW..." Our salvation and place in God's family is so important that God does not want us wishing that we have eternal life, or hoping that we have eternal life. No, he wants us to KNOW with certainty that we have eternal life. He also wants us to know that our eternal life has already started. He does not say, "...know that you will have eternal life." No, in Christ, we already have eternal life. What a wonderful thing to be set on a table before us – complete assurance. This kind of assurance, this kind of knowledge, can only come by revelation from God. As Romans 8:16 says:

The Spirit himself testifies with our spirit that we are God's children.

Making It Real:
So let me ask you, is this foundation of peace and order written on your heart? Do you know that you are a child of God, perfectly forgiven and on your way to heaven? Do you know that you have already received eternal life? The Lord, who is your generous host, places perfect assurance on the table before you.
Have you seen it?
Do you know it?
Are you living it?

▌ *Have you thanked him for it?*

So God prepares a table for me, a table for you, but it is not just FOR you, it is BEFORE you, and there is a significant difference. We know that when Jesus returns there will be a banquet in heaven, and we could say that God is preparing a "table" for us for that future time. I imagine that we'll turn up and it will be already laid out, already prepared. But the sense here is very different, because the word used for "before me" here can mean face or in front of my face (22), or we might say "before my eyes". So the picture here is not like when you arrive at a party and the host has already arranged all the food on the table for you. The picture is that you arrive as a guest, and the host says, "Welcome, come and sit at my table, make yourself at home." And then bit by bit he starts to bring things to the table, bit by bit he orders and arranges things in front of your eyes. This is how God brings order to our lives, piece by piece, gradually, over a period of time, before our eyes. What is the Lord arranging on the table before your eyes at this time in your life? Ask him to show you, look for it.

IN THE PRESENCE OF MY ENEMIES?

There's something else quite remarkable about the way that our God, our generous host, prepares a table for us - it is in the presence of our enemies. What does that mean? It means that God blesses us and orders our lives every day, even when life feels hard and hostile. The word for enemies here is actually a verb, and it means to show hostility toward someone, to harass, to oppress, to afflict, to bind up (23). Have you felt harassed, oppressed or afflicted recently? The lesson from this verse is that we don't have to focus on the annoyance, the oppression, the harassment, the danger, or the hostility; we can focus instead on what God is preparing for us. How much more joy and peace will be ours if we do. God does not keep his blessing for the good times, he pours out his blessing ALL the time, even in the middle of life's trials, even in the presence of my enemies.

> *Making It Real:*
> *Do you feel like you are waiting for God's blessing? If you do, stop waiting, and look at the table he is arranging before your eyes. Whether you are rejoicing or heart broken, let me encourage you to look for the good and thank him, even in the presence of your enemies.*

YOU ANOINT MY HEAD WITH OIL

But your generous host doesn't stop there, because he anoints your head with oil. Now in our culture we might not thank someone for pouring oil on our head, especially if we had washed our hair for a special occasion. But in Bible times it was an act of courtesy towards an honoured guest, who had journeyed to a feast under the burning sun. It brought a sense of comfort and refreshment. As Psalm 104 says:

He makes ...oil to make their faces shine.

In Luke 7:46 Jesus said to a less than generous host:

You did not put oil on my head, but she has poured perfume on my feet.

You are God's honoured guest; he wants to refresh you. If you have put your trust in Jesus to save you, you have entered eternal life by the main entrance, not sneaked in by the back door. There is no back door. So I'll say it again, you are God's honoured guest. As oil might trickle down your head, so let the love and honour that God has shown you trickle into your being, let it refresh your soul.

Oil often symbolises the Holy Spirit, and God has given us the Holy Spirit to renew and empower us:

he saved us, not because of righteous things we had done, but because of his mercy. He saved us through the washing of rebirth and renewal by the Holy Spirit, WHOM HE POURED OUT ON US GENEROUSLY through Jesus Christ our Saviour, so that, having been justified by his grace, we might become heirs having the hope of eternal life. (Titus 3:5-7)

God has not given us just a dab of Holy Spirit, like some perfume. No, he has been extravagant in his generosity, drenching us with all the fullness of his Spirit. Which brings me to another one of my favourite verses about God's generosity towards us:

In him we have redemption through his blood, the forgiveness of sins, in accordance with the riches of God's grace that he lavished on us with all wisdom and understanding. (Ephesians 1:7,8)

Here we see how God has lavished his grace on us, again displaying his boundless generosity towards us. But what I love about this is the way that Paul adds, "with all wisdom and understanding". God did not make a mistake when he forgave me so freely and fully, his hand didn't slip as he was sprinkling his grace on me and gave me too much by accident. No, he did it with the full knowledge of what he was doing and the full knowledge of everything that I would do in the future. He fully understood all the ways I would fail him and let him down, and he still lavished his grace on me, just like he has lavished his grace on you.

A NEW PERSPECTIVE

So is there any wonder, going back to Psalm 23, that David finishes the verse by summing up his picture of God as his generous host by saying, "my cup overflows". Now there are supposed to be two kinds of people in the world, "glass half full" people and "glass half empty" people. But David is neither of these, he is a "glass overflowing" person. He has a perspective on life that most people just don't see. It is as if he's saying, "When I consider how you have honoured me with all your generous love and provision, it's too much Lord, it's too much. How can I ever come near to containing it let alone being worthy of it?"

And I suppose that is the point. We certainly are not worthy of his love, none of us are. And we are not supposed to keep his generosity to ourselves; we are to let it flow out from us to the people around us. In Matthew 10:8, as he sent out his disciples, Jesus said:

'Freely you have received; freely give.'

Freely you have received, freely give! Are we generously giving what God has given so generously to us? Do you want to change your perspective to a "glass overflowing" person? If so, look at what God, your saviour and generous host, is arranging before you.

ARE YOU GOING TO SERVE ME?

There's one more surprising thing to me about this verse – If God is our generous host, bringing order and peace to our lives, honouring us with refreshing oil and pouring out so much blessing that we can't contain it, then it is God who is serving us. But surely, it's supposed to be the other way around, aren't we supposed to be serving him? Of course, we are supposed to be serving him, but the wonder of our relationship with him, and the marvel of his love is that while we are serving him, he is also serving us. What is pictured for us here in Psalm 23 is demonstrated for us by Jesus when he washed the disciples' feet. John 13:3-15 says:

> Jesus knew that the Father had put all things under his power, and that he had come from God and was returning to God; so he got up from the meal, took off his outer clothing, and wrapped a towel round his waist. After that, he poured water into a basin and began to wash his disciples' feet, drying them with the towel that was wrapped round him.
> He came to Simon Peter, who said to him, 'Lord, are you going to wash my feet?'

Jesus replied, 'You do not realise now what I am doing, but later you will understand.'

'No,' said Peter, 'you shall never wash my feet.'

Jesus answered, 'Unless I wash you, you have no part with me.'

'Then, Lord,' Simon Peter replied, 'not just my feet but my hands and my head as well!'

Jesus answered, 'Those who have had a bath need only to wash their feet; their whole body is clean. And you are clean, though not every one of you.' For he knew who was going to betray him, and that was why he said not every one was clean.

When he had finished washing their feet, he put on his clothes and returned to his place. 'Do you understand what I have done for you?' he asked them. 'You call me "Teacher" and "Lord", and rightly so, for that is what I am. Now that I, your Lord and Teacher, have washed your feet, you also should wash one another's feet. I have set you an example that you should do as I have done for you.

Jesus the Lord of the universe became a servant as an example to us. No pretence, no care for position, he just served those he loved, and he serves them still. By his grace, he even serves you and me as our generous host.

Making It Real:
How can we follow Jesus' example? By giving what he has given to us. Is God bringing order and peace to your life? Seek order and peace in your relationships with others. Is he helping you

in your hour of need? Help others in theirs. Have you had grace and mercy lavished upon you? Lavish grace and mercy on others. Have you been freely forgiven? Make sure you freely forgive. Have you received honour from the Lord of Lords? Give honour to all that you meet.

Is your cup overflowing? Freely you have received; freely give.

6. HOPE FOR TOMORROW

Surely goodness and love will follow me
all the days of my life,
and I will dwell in the house of the Lord
for ever. (Psalm 23:6)

Hope is really, really important. When I was younger, I did not understand this. When the apostle Paul wrote "these three remain, faith, hope and love" (1 Corinthians 13:13), I could completely understand why faith and love were so important, but hope puzzled me. I think it was for two reasons:

1. I was young, and didn't understand very much about life
2. Being a naturally optimistic person, I thought hope was a constant part of everyone's life.

Now I'm older and have seen more of life, I understand that hope is as essential to the human soul, as air is to breathing. Without hope we are lost. Martin Luther said:

Everything that is done in the world is done by hope.

A Canadian organisation, called Bellwood Health Services, helps in the treatment of addiction, and goes as far as to say that, "Hope…is the bedrock upon which you build your recovery." (24) Hope creates motivation; motivation leads to action; and action produces change. This is true of recovery from addiction and it's true of every action we take. To paraphrase Martin Luther – without hope nothing gets done, nothing changes.

What's even more amazing about the kind of hope referred to in the Bible, is that it's not hope in the sense of, "I hope the weather is good for my holiday next week." This kind of hope is expressing a wish for something to happen, but there is very little certainty that it will. But the Greek word for hope used by the apostle Paul in 1 Corinthians 13:13, and fifty three times in the New Testament means hope in the sense of "expectation of what is sure" (25). This Christian perspective takes hope to a whole new level. The key question is – where does this kind of hope come from?

WHERE DOES HOPE COME FROM?

In our journey through Psalm 23 we have come to the last verse, and here David tells us where his hope comes from. In verse 6 he says:

> Surely goodness and love will follow me
>   all the days of my life,
> and I will dwell in the house of the Lord
>   for ever.

Up until this point in Psalm 23, David has been focused on the here and now, his daily experience of God. Up to this point he has described everything in the present tense: The Lord IS my shepherd; he LEADS me; he RESTORES my soul; he GUIDES me; you ARE with me. But he ends the Psalm by looking forward; he ends by describing his hope for tomorrow.

He starts the end of his Psalm with the word SURELY! Surely is a very positive word isn't it? It is full of confidence, and leaves no room for doubt. It is positive, assertive and certain about what is to follow.

Now, there are some words or phrases in the world of legal jargon that make me smile. One of the words is "plurality". You don't hear that word every day, do you. Plurality is a word often used in Patent applications to describe more than one of something, like a plurality of cars. As I say, it just makes me smile. I guess I'm easily amused. But there is another phrase that is used in legal contracts that makes me smile too, and it is this:

For the avoidance of doubt…

Picture the scene – I'm sitting at work, with my elbows on the desk and my chin on my hand, reading a long legal contract that goes on and on in minute detail about all sorts of stuff that is hard to understand and will probably never happen, turning over page after page, when suddenly I come to a paragraph that starts with the words, "For the avoidance of doubt…", and then a smile comes on my face. Why? Because I know that what comes next will be important and will bring clarity - I love clarity. Why they don't just keep all the "For avoidance of doubt…" paragraphs and bin the rest is beyond me.

Anyway, my point is this – in starting his last verse of Psalm 23 with the word "Surely", David has turned this verse into a "For the avoidance of doubt…" verse. He is saying, "For the avoidance of doubt, goodness and love will follow me all the days of my life, and I will dwell in the house of the Lord for ever." That makes me smile, and I hope that it makes you smile too. This is a verse upon which we can build our hope.

AVOIDING DOUBT

But it's one thing to say, "For the avoidance of doubt..." it's another thing to avoid doubt in our thoughts and feelings. So how do we avoid doubt? Well I think it boils down to three words: hope, faith and confidence. It's one thing to hope for something, it's quite another to be confident about it. Hebrews 11:1 says:

Now faith is <u>confidence</u> in what we hope for and assurance about what we do not see.

Confidence – what an important word that is! Would you rather be full of confidence or full of doubt? Reading that verse, the mathematician in me wants to express it as:

Faith = Confidence + Hope

If you add confidence to hope the result is faith. In fact, we know that we have faith about something, if we feel confident about it.

There's one more thing about this word confidence that I think is helpful to understand - confidence comes from the Latin word "cōnfīdō", which comes from two other words: "con", meaning "with" + "fīdō", meaning "trust" (26). Confidence means "with trust", and what is faith if it is not about trust? Is our faith in Jesus Christ not built on our trust in him, is it not built on our trust in the power of his death and resurrection to save us?

Of course, people can have confidence because they are trusting in all sorts of things. An athlete cannot compete in the Olympics without a lot of confidence, but what is that confidence based on? Is it based on their natural ability? Is it based on their training and hard work? Is it based on using performance enhancing drugs? Christian Olympians put their confidence somewhere else, they put their confidence in God. The US Olympic football player Morgan Brian is quoted as saying, "Playing is a chance to put trust in God" (27). That's a great perspective, and as followers of Jesus we can have that perspective too.

> *Making It Real:*
> *You and I can say, "Living, working, waiting, serving, is a chance to put trust in God". We can say every morning, "Today is a chance to put trust in God."*

CONFIDENT ABOUT TOMORROW

So, here are two questions for you and me:

1) How confident are you feeling right now?
2) What is your confidence based on?

I guess the answer depends on the area of life we are talking about. If I ask you whether you are confident that the sun will rise tomorrow, you will probably say yes, and your confidence will be based on past history. But if I ask you, are you confident about the future, your answer might be quite different, after all, none of us know what the future might hold.

And yet it is precisely the future that David is confident about in Psalm 23. He is confident that goodness and love will follow him all the days of his life. The word for "goodness" means beautiful, best, bountiful and cheerful (28), and the word for "love" means loving-kindness, favour and mercy (29). David was confident that his future would not only contain these things, but that they would follow him. Now the meaning here is not "follow" as in the sense of lagging behind like some sulking child. Perhaps it can feel like that sometimes, as if we're waiting for goodness to catch us up, thinking, "Come on goodness, where are you when I need you? Keep up!"

No, the meaning here is that goodness is chasing after us and that love is hunting us down (30). Just let that sink in for a minute. It just amazes me to think that goodness is not just some disinterested onlooker in my life, who is following me reluctantly, but instead it is like a bloodhound hunting me down, thinking, "How can I bring goodness to him in this situation?"

> *Making It Real:*
> *How does it feel to be hunted by goodness and love, not just some days, but ALL days – "...all the days of my life"? There is not a single day in your future when God will not be seeking you out to*

> *give you goodness, to give you love, even in those times, when you walk through the darkest valley. David doesn't say that there won't be pain; he doesn't say that there won't be trouble and distress, but he DOES say that there will always be goodness, there will always be love, there will always be kindness, hot on your heels.*

John Ortberg writes in his book "Soul Keeping" that his mentor Dallas Willard once said, "The gospel means that the universe is a perfectly safe place for you to be." "It means", he says, "that the soul is simply not at risk. Not even from cancer. What else could Paul have meant when he said nothing can separate us from the love of God? Why else would Jesus have advised us not to worry?" (31)

Do you feel safe? It's hard to feel confident if you don't feel safe. David felt confident about the future because he felt safe in the care of his shepherd. David understood one thousand years before the apostle Paul that nothing could separate him from the love of God.

DWELLING IN THE HOUSE OF THE LORD FOR EVER

David then goes on to say, "and I will dwell in the house of the Lord for ever." He ends his meditation on the Lord as his shepherd and generous host, by looking to his journey's end, to his final destination – the house of the Lord. What is the house of the Lord but the place where God dwells? And since God is love and God is light, it will literally be heaven to be there. I wince a little inside when I hear someone say, "It's to die for", about some experience in life, or place to be, or thing to possess, because I think, "Really? To die for?" But Heaven, to dwell in the house of the Lord for ever, now that is to die for.

Death is rather a taboo subject in our culture, we tend to ignore it until it is staring us in the face through a sudden realisation of our own mortality, or that of a loved one. But for Christians, death need hold no fear. We might not be looking forward to the process, but the end result is heaven. Having that sure hope of heaven is the ultimate confidence in life, because we can know that no matter what happens, we will dwell with our shepherd forever.

What does it mean to dwell somewhere? It means to sit down, to settle. In this life, we are just passing through. We might feel our home is permanent, but it's really only temporary. We are all living in the equivalent of caravans, no matter how big or small, because our real home, our permanent dwelling place is in heaven. Are you confident of heaven, or are you just hoping in a wishing sense? God wants us to be confident. He wants us to know that we have eternal life, to know that the Lord my shepherd will lead me home.

HOW TO LIVE WITH HOPE FOR TOMORROW

> *Making It Real:*
> *So then, how can we apply all this to our lives? Well I think it can be expressed in three states of being that Romans 12:12 summarises for us, "Be joyful in hope, patient in affliction, faithful in prayer."*

1.   Be joyful in hope.

Our shepherd wants us to be joyful in hope. How is your joy right now? There are two subtle yet powerful enemies of joy that we all battle with: comparison and worry. Whenever we compare ourselves to others, we allow our joy to be stolen. Our nature tends to home in on those that seem better off than us, and the result is dissatisfaction. Try being joyful in hope when you are feeling dissatisfied. The tenth commandment says, "You shall not covet" (Exodus 20:17), in part, because it steals our joy.

And then there's worry. Can you be joyful and worry at the same time? No, worry steals your joy, and worry has to do with uncertainty about the future, but if we know that goodness and love will always follow us, why do we worry? Is that not why Jesus said, "Do not worry about tomorrow" (Matthew 6:34)? And yet we do. Worry affects us in different ways. When I'm facing uncertainty about the future, what I've realised, and my wife can testify to, is that worry makes me grumpy and intolerant. But what I've also realised, is that these uncertainties are really opportunities; they are opportunities to trust God. They are, like the Olympian said, a chance to put trust in God.

2.   Be patient in affliction.

Can you be joyful in hope and patient in affliction at the same time? I think you can, but it is a challenge. As Dallas Willard once said to John Ortberg as he faced a great affliction in his life, "This will be a test of your joyful confidence in God." (31) Worrying about stuff that hasn't happened robs us of our joy, but so can affliction when it does happen, and it happens to all of us, sooner or later. But actually, if we face suffering with trust in our shepherd, then it will increase our hope. As Romans 5:3-5 says:

> Not only so, but we also glory in our sufferings, because we know that suffering produces perseverance; perseverance, character; and character, hope. And hope does not put us to shame...

Hoping in the Lord our shepherd will never put us to shame, has he not promised that goodness and love will follow us always? If there will be any shame or regret, it will be from our lack of hope, it will be from our lack of trust.

3. Be faithful in prayer

I think that Psalm 23:6 gives us a great place to start in praying for others, as well as for ourselves. If we know God's promise of goodness and love, then we can pray that goodness and love into someone's life, into the specifics of their situation. And remember this is a promise for you too, goodness and love will follow YOU all the days of YOUR life, so let this stir faith in you as you make your requests to God.

For the avoidance of doubt, goodness and love will follow you all the days of your life, and you will dwell in the house of the Lord for ever.

Dear reader, I'd like to proclaim this blessing over your life:

May the God of hope fill you with all joy and peace as you trust in him, so that you may overflow with hope by the power of the Holy Spirit. (Romans 15:13)

Amen!

7. THE PSALM 23 LIFE

So, we've taken time to consider the meaning of some familiar words, but how familiar is our experience of these words? David's experience of the goodness of God, just oozes contentment and joy. He describes for us the Psalm 23 life that is:

- A life lived in confidence and certainty for the present and the future.
- A life that trusts in the Shepherd's care, a care based on his perfect knowledge of you.
- A life of a sheep that, having gone astray, has been found and rescued by the Good Shepherd.
- A life that is content to say, "The Lord as my Shepherd, what more do I need."
- A life lived in complete safety, punctuated by rest that restores my soul.
- A life free from fear, even in the presence of deep trouble and trial; a life free from worry.
- A life focused on the journey, because the destination is secure.

- A life called to follow my Shepherd along paths of righteous that will glorify him, knowing that it's all about him and not about me.
- A life lived with joyful confidence in God and his overflowing blessings.
- A life that takes every chance to trust my Saviour.
- A life lived in the confident knowledge of God's eternal love for me.

This last feature of the Psalm 23 life is, as has been suggested already, the most important thing that any one of us needs to know. God's love, and the way it is expressed to us, is the core theme of Psalm 23.

Indeed, recognising and acknowledging with sincere thanks and praise, God's love that endures for ever is central to his plan of redemption, because as David Gooding points out:

> The issue at stake has always been - at least since Eden - the validity or otherwise of Satan's slander that put into question not God's power but his love. That slander has penetrated and poisoned the human race ever since. It is the mainstay of the power of darkness over men's minds still. By definition it could not be settled by any exhibition of miraculous power, however stupendous. Power by itself could have everyone grovelling in terror, or open-mouthed with wonder, at the Almighty's strength; but power by itself could never convert the human heart from suspicion, disobedience, proud independence and

fear, to love, trust, gratitude, and obedience to God. Only Almighty love could do that. And Calvary was the place where that love was forever demonstrated beyond all question. (15)

As the apostle Paul puts it:

But God demonstrates his own love for us in this: While we were still sinners, Christ died for us. (Romans 5:8)

ANOTHER RELATIONSHIP

While the central theme of scripture is God's redeeming love, expressed most fully in the Gospel of our Lord Jesus Christ, the glory of Psalm 23 is the way that it expresses the love of God in our everyday life and experience – the Psalm 23 life. Such a life can belong to those who have made Jesus Christ their Lord and Saviour. And yet who of us can say that they possess such a life in its entirety? David used the relationship of a shepherd with his sheep, and a generous host with his guest, as the closest things in his experience, to express the impact of God's goodness and love on his life. And yet, as true and as wonderful as these relationships are, viewed from this side of the Cross, they were but a foretaste of what was yet to come. To those who, by the grace of God, have been born again by the Spirit of God, there is an immeasurably more wonderful relationship given, not just as a picture, but as a reality:

See what great love the Father has lavished on us, that we should be called children of God! And that is what we are! (1 John 3:1)

The Father, out of his boundless love, calls us his children. He sees us, and treats us, as his children, because we have been born again by the Spirit of God, through his grace. We are much more to him than sheep, much more than honoured guests, we are children and heirs with Christ. This fact has implications for our future that we cannot now comprehend. As 1 John 3:2 goes on to say:

Dear friends, now we are children of God, and what we will be has not yet been made known. But we know that when Christ appears, we shall be like him, for we shall see him as he is.

Such is the nature, for now, of dwelling in the house of the Lord for ever.

Our present focus, however, is on Psalm 23 and the life experience it lays before us. If David could experience the love of God in this way, how much more can we as children of God? And so, the question before us is this – how can I make the Psalm 23 life a greater, and growing, reality in my everyday life?

ENTERING IN

The realisation that, thanks to the Cross of Christ, those who believe in Jesus have become Children of God, gives us more than a hint of how to enter fully into the Psalm 23 life.

When Jesus was on Earth he talked often about the "kingdom of God", or "the kingdom of heaven", as being something near and present, as well as something yet to come. The Psalm 23 life describes only part, but nevertheless, an essential part of what living in the kingdom of God means for his children – what his children can expect to experience now, as part of their birthright. Jesus used the example of a little child to show not only how to enter, but also how to live in the kingdom of heaven:

> At that time the disciples came to Jesus and asked, 'Who, then, is the greatest in the kingdom of heaven?'
> He called a little child to him, and placed the child among them. And he said: 'Truly I tell you, unless you change and become like little children, you will never enter the kingdom of heaven. Therefore, whoever takes the lowly position of this child is the greatest in the kingdom of heaven.' (Matthew 18:1-4)

So the disciples wanted to know who was the greatest in the kingdom of heaven, a question that revealed how little they understood at that point in time. In reply Jesus calls a little child to him, and says, 'Truly I tell you, unless

115

you change and become like little children, you will never enter the kingdom of heaven.' Now the disciples were adults, so what does it mean for an adult to become like a little child? Our granddaughter Ruth, at the point where she was just learning to take her first steps, taught me two important lessons on this.

The first lesson was her total dependence. She could not walk without help. She needed someone to hold her hand, or even both hands. But I noticed something about this, she was not unhappy about needing help, she did not resent needing help, in fact she was very happy to receive help. She didn't seem to give needing help a second thought, it was just natural to her. She was focused on exploring and learning, and she welcomed and expected help to do it. I realised that at that age children have no pride, they have no ego, that could get in the way of receiving help. Little children are people who are totally dependent beings, who are very happy to be so. Unless we gladly accept our total dependence on God, we will never enter the kingdom of heaven, let alone possess it. Do you gladly accept your total dependence on God, or are you still trying to show the world that you can do it on your own?

So Ruth could not walk without help, but the second lesson I learned was this – neither could she walk unless she took the steps. We could hold her hands all day, but unless she decided to put one foot in front of the other, she could not walk. This is the best illustration I know, of how our relationship with God is supposed to work. We follow Jesus in total dependence upon him, recognising that without him we can do nothing, but at the same time, we do the walking. In one sense we walk into the kingdom of heaven by taking the step of acknowledging our total dependence on God, that our good deeds are bankrupt, and that all we have to offer are filthy rags. Jesus then carries us across the threshold, and we are born again by the Spirit of God. If you have never acknowledged your total dependence on God, then let today be the day that you do.

July 4th is Independence Day, when Americans celebrate their Declaration of Independence. Let today be the day that you make your "Declaration of Dependence" on almighty God, and Jesus Christ his Son. Let today be your "Dependence Day".

Making It Real:
When trials come, when we walk through the dark valley, our weakness becomes clear to us, and declaring our dependence on God is somehow easier to do. Are you facing a situation in your life which is calling for you to declare your dependence on God? Let today be your "Declaration of Dependence" day. Or perhaps you are on a roll – life is working well, and your hopes and plans are being fulfilled. In such times we can feel that we don't need any help, and our dependence is much harder to see. If that is you, then praise God, for what do you have that you did not receive (1 Corinthians 4:7). Let me encourage you too, let today be your "Declaration of Dependence" day.

Now, children grow up and rightly become independent. So, once we become a Christian and are in the kingdom of heaven, then do we as Christians grow out of our need to be like a little child? As we grow in Christ, as our Heavenly Father intends that we should, do we not become mature and beyond childish ways? Well yes, it is certainly true that God has given us the Holy Spirit precisely to enable us to become mature - more and more like Jesus, but we must become mature and remain a little child at the same time. In fact, I cannot be mature in Christ, if I do not at the same time also see myself as a little child before God. To do otherwise would be to fall into the devil's trap.

Jesus said to his disciples, "whoever takes the lowly position of this child is the greatest in the kingdom of heaven" (Matthew 18:4). So, having entered the kingdom by being like a little child, in total dependence on God, those who are greatest in the kingdom remain like a little child, they remain totally dependent on God. Even the incarnate Son of God said:

Very truly I tell you, the Son can do nothing by himself; he can do only what he sees his Father doing, because whatever the Father does the Son also does. (John 5:19)

You see, in the Garden of Eden we were made originally to walk with God in total dependence and joy. Sin entered the world when Adam and Eve chose the path of independence from God. The devil tempted Eve into taking that path, he lied to her, and he is lying to us still. In our daily life he whispers in our ear things like, "You don't need to bother God about this; he's far too busy to be interested in your daily life; you've got this far, you can do this on your own."

And if you want to serve God, which as you mature you certainly will, then the devil will whisper things like, "You've done this many times; you're not a baby Christian anymore, you can do this; it's time you showed what you can do." He even whispers things like, "God needs you to do this, how will he do it if you don't?" These are the most dangerous lies because, just like his lie to Eve, these are half-truths, they are lies with a spot of truth added. Yes, God chooses to work through us, his children, and that will require sacrifice, but to think that we are somehow doing God a favour, that somehow if we don't summon up the strength to do this, then the plans of Almighty God will be stopped dead in their tracks, is foolish indeed. It would be rather like a one-year old thinking, "Unless I help Mummy, or Daddy, make dinner, they won't be able to do it." Mummy, or Daddy, may allow the child to help, because it is good for the child and a joy to them, not because they need the help!

There is a book called "God Can Do It Without Me", which is a personal testimony of recovering from burn out. Am I trying to encourage you to serve God less? No!

Making It Real:
What I am encouraging you to do is question the basis upon which you are serving God. Are you serving God like a little child, in total dependence on him, or is there some ego

119

> *creeping in, some sense of entitlement after all the sacrifices you have made, some sense of superiority, or greatness, because of your spiritual achievements?*

LIVING THE PSALM 23 LIFE

So how does becoming like a little child help us to live in the full reality of the Psalm 23 life? God's love is so great that we cannot even begin to measure it, and it is so firm that it lasts forever. All we need to do is remember his love every day; and we remember his love by receiving it; and we receive his love by declaring our dependence upon it. Therefore, as dearly loved children let us make our "Declaration of Dependence" on the love of God every day.

There is a four-word phrase that is repeated forty-three times in the Old Testament. It is used during the dedication of the temple of the Lord built by Solomon, and it is used thirty five times in the Psalms, and twenty six times in one Psalm in particular, Psalm 136 – the phrase is:

His love endures forever.

Psalm 136 is mainly a list of things that God has done, and after each short statement the Psalmist declares, "His love endures forever", to underline the fact that everything God has done comes from his eternal love. Let me encourage you to declare these four words often in your life, for they are true, and they declare our total opposition to the devil's slander, that cast doubt on God's love for us.

So, declare your dependence on God, declare his love for you that endures forever, and finally give thanks to The Lord. There is nothing you have done, or could do, to deserve his love. He loves you, because he loves you. He loves you, because God is love. May the Psalm 23 life be yours now and always.

To underline Psalm 23 as a description of God's love for you, I'd like to give it the Psalm 136 treatment:

The Lord is my shepherd, I shall not be in want.

His love endures forever.

He makes me lie down in green pastures,
    he leads me beside quiet waters,
he restores my soul.

His love endures forever.

He guides me in paths of righteousness
    for his name's sake.

His love endures forever.

Even though I walk
    through the valley of the shadow of death,
I will fear no evil,

for you are with me;
your rod and your staff,
    they comfort me.

Your love endures forever.

You prepare a table before me
    in the presence of my enemies.

Your love endures forever.

You anoint my head with oil;
    my cup overflows.

Your love endures forever.

Surely goodness and love will follow me
    all the days of my life,
and I will dwell in the house of the Lord
    forever.

HIS LOVE ENDURES FOREVER!

SOURCES

1. Petersen, Jonathan. Bible Gateway 2019 on Parade. *BibleGateway.* [Online] 26 December 2019. [Cited: 19 May 2020.] https://www.biblegateway.com/blog/2019/12/bible-gateway-2019-on-parade/.

2. 2019 in Review. *BibleGateway.* [Online] 2019. [Cited: 19 May 2020.] https://www.biblegateway.com/year-in-review/2019/.

3. Willard, Dallas. *The Allure of Gentleness: Defending the Faith in the Manner of Jesus.* s.l. : HarperOne, 2015.

4. Wight, Fred H. *Manner And Customs of Bible Lands.* 1953.

5. McLeod, Saul. Maslow's Hierarchy of Needs. *SimplyPsychology.* [Online] 20th March 2020. [Cited: 19th April 2020.] https://www.simplypsychology.org/maslow.html.

6. Graham, Billy. If you find a perfect church don't join it: You'd spoil it. *AZ Quotes.* [Online] [Cited: 27 June 2020.] https://www.azquotes.com/quote/697892.

7. Strong's Concordance. *Bible Hub.* [Online] [Cited: 4 July 2020.] https://biblehub.com/hebrew/2637.htm.

8. Strong's Concordance. *Bible Hub.* [Online] [Cited: 4 July 2020.] https://biblehub.com/hebrew/4999.htm.

9. Strong's Concordance. *Bible Hub.* [Online] [Cited: 4 July 2020.] https://biblehub.com/hebrew/5095.htm.

10. Strong's Concordance. *Bible Hub.* [Online] [Cited: 4 July 2020.] https://biblehub.com/hebrew/4496.htm.

11. MacDonald, Gordon. *Ordering Your Private World.* Crowborough : Highland Books, 1987.

12. Spafford, Horatio G. It Is Well with My Soul. *Timeless Truths.* [Online] [Cited: 19th April 2020.] https://library.timelesstruths.org/music/It_Is_Well_with_My_Soul/.

13. guide. *Dictionary.com.* [Online] [Cited: 4 July 2020.] https://www.dictionary.com/browse/guide.

14. Definition of righteousness noun from the Oxford Advanced Learner's Dictionary. *Oxford Learner's Dictionary.* [Online] [Cited: 4 July 2020.] https://www.oxfordlearnersdictionaries.com/definition/english/righteousness.

15. Gooding, David. *True to the Faith.* s.l. : Myrtlefield House, 2013.

16. Strong's Concordance. *Bible Hub.* [Online] https://biblehub.com/hebrew/6757.htm.

17. Strong's Concordance. *Bible Hub.* [Online] [Cited: 4 July 2020.] https://biblehub.com/hebrew/7451.htm.

18. Ebenezer. *Dictionary.com.* [Online] [Cited: 12 July 2020.] https://www.dictionary.com/browse/ebenezer.

19. Strong's Concordance. *Bible Hub.* [Online] [Cited: 5 July 2020.] https://biblehub.com/hebrew/4938.htm.

20. Hammerstein, Oscar. You'll Never Walk Alone - lyrics. 1945.

21. Strong's Concordance. *Bible Hub.* [Online] [Cited: 5 July 2020.] https://biblehub.com/hebrew/6186.htm.

22. Strong's Concordance. *Bible Hub.* [Online] [Cited: 5 July 2020.] https://biblehub.com/hebrew/6440.htm.

23. Strong's Concordance. *Bible Hub.* [Online] [Cited: 5 July 2020.] https://biblehub.com/hebrew/6887.htm.

24. Ratnanather, George. The Importance of Hope in Addiction Recovery. *Edgewood Health Network.* [Online] 5 March 2014. [Cited: 19 May 2020.] https://www.edgewoodhealthnetwork.com/blog/the-importance-of-hope-in-addiction-recovery/.

25. Strong's Concordance. *Bible Hub.* [Online] [Cited: 4 July 2020.] https://biblehub.com/greek/1680.htm.

26. Confidence. *Wiktionary.* [Online] [Cited: 5 July 2020.] https://en.wiktionary.org/wiki/confidence.

27. Sells, Heather. Soccer's Morgan Brian: Playing Is a Chance to Put Trust in God. *CBNNEWS.COM.* [Online] CBN, 11 August 2016. [Cited: 19 May 2020.] https://www1.cbn.com/cbnnews/us/2016/august/olympic-soccer-star-says-playing-is-a-chance-to-put-trust-in-god.

28. Strong's Exhaustive Concordance. *Bible Hub.* [Online] [Cited: 5 July 2020.] https://biblehub.com/hebrew/2896.htm.

29. Strong's Concordance. *Bible Hub.* [Online] [Cited: 5 July 2020.] https://biblehub.com/hebrew/2617.htm.

30. Strong's Concordance. *Bible Hub.* [Online] [Cited: 5 July 2020.] https://biblehub.com/hebrew/7291.htm.

31. Ortberg, John. *Soul Keeping: Caring For the Most Important Part of You.* s.l. : Zondervan, 2014.

32. Hunte, Todd D. *Our Character at Work: Success from the Heart of Servant Leadership.* s.l. : Wheatmark, 2016.

ABOUT THE AUTHOR

David Knott responded to the call to follow Jesus as an engineering student. He worked for a world leading aerospace company for thirty-nine years, and is a Chartered Mechanical Engineer and Fellow of the Institute of Mechanical Engineers. He has an internal drive to understand, whether it is the physics of aerodynamics, or the nature of our relationship with God. He has been a Bible teacher for over thirty years, and a Church Elder, his passion being to help others understand scripture's vital truth, apply it, and be inwardly transformed in the process.

He now trains and facilitates others in how to generate inventions and solve difficult problems.

He has been married to his wife Kathryn for nearly forty years. They have two married children, and one granddaughter.

Printed in Great Britain
by Amazon